P9-DGH-850

And I Know He Watches Me

Sandy Lynam Clough

HARVEST HOUSE PUBLISHERS
Eugene, Oregon

And I Know He Watches Me

Copyright © 1999 Sandy Lynam Clough
Published by Harvest House Publishers
Eugene, Oregon 97402

Library of Congress Cataloging-in-Publication Data

Clough, Sandy Lynam, 1948-
    And I know he watches me / Sandy Lynam Clough.
        p.   cm.
    ISBN 1-56507-988-4
    1. Clough, Sandy Lynam, 1948-   .   2. Artists—United States-
-Biography.   3. Visually handicapped—United States—Biography.
4. Christian Biography—United States.   5. Consolation.   I. Title.
BR1725.C526A3   1999
248.8'6'092—dc21
    [b]   98-38534
                                                              CIP

Design and production by Garborg Design Works, Minneapolis, Minnesota

Unless otherwise noted, Scripture quotations are taken from the New American Standard Bible, © 1960, 1962, 1963, 1968, 1971, 1972, 1973, 1975, 1977 by The Lockman Foundation. Used by permission.
Verses marked AMP are taken from The Amplified Bible, Old Testament, Copyright © 1965 and 1987 by The Zondervan Corporation, and from The Amplified New Testament, Copyright © 1954, 1958, 1987 by the Lockman Foundation. Used by permission.
Verses marked TLB are taken from The Living Bible, Copyright © 1971 owned by assignment by Illinois Regional Bank N.A. (as trustee). Used by permission of Tyndale House Publishers, Inc., Wheaton, Illinois 60189. All rights reserved.
Verses marked NIV are taken from the Holy Bible, New International Version, Copyright © 1973, 1978, 1984 by the International Bible Society. Used by permission of Zondervan Publishing House.

"Deep Water"—words and music by Kevin Harris, copyright © 1997 Fresh Music, Tampa, Florida. (813) 989-8712. Used by permission.

"Draw Me"—words and music copyright © 1998 Randy Newton. (770) 427-6137. Used by permission.

Printed in the United States of America.

99 00 01 02 03 04 05 06 07 08 /BG/ 10 9 8 7 6 5 4 3

To every person who has prayed for me

and for my healing—

Many of you I know so well

and some of you I have never met.

In my darkest days, you were the reason

I knew the Lord

had not forgotten me.

I am indebted to your amazing love.

His Eye Is On the Sparrow

Mrs. L. D. Martin and Charles H. Gabriel

Why should I feel discouraged, why should the shadows come,
Why should my heart be lonely and long for Heav'n and home,
When Jesus is my portion? My constant friend is He;
His eye is on the sparrow, and I know He watches me;
His eye is on the sparrow, and I know He watches me.

"Let not your heart be troubled," His tender word I hear,
And resting on His goodness I lose my doubt and fears;
Tho' by the path He leadeth but one step I may see;
His eye is on the sparrow, and I know He watches me.
His eye is on the sparrow, and I know He watches me.

Whenever I am tempted, whenever clouds arise,
When songs give place to sighing, when hope within me dies,
I draw the closer to Him, from care He sets me free;
His eye is on the sparrow, and I know He cares for me;
His eye is on the sparrow, and I know He cares for me.

I sing because I'm happy,
    I sing because I'm free,
For His eye is on the sparrow,
    and I know He watches me.

And I Know He Watches Me

I had been plucked out of my busy schedule and placed on a shelf for weeks. Life went on around me while I sat, not knowing what my outcome would be. Since the doctors wouldn't allow me to read, the only comfort from God's Word came from what I could remember. Watching television, I heard someone singing "His Eye Is On the Sparrow." I was surprised when a voice spoke to my heart, "You are precious to Him." How I needed that expression of God's love!

When my situation got worse and I faced frightening surgery, my longtime friend Gerrie called with a verse the Lord had given her for me: "Do not fear; you are of more value than many sparrows" (Matthew 10:31). After talking to the Lord so much about my own eyes, but not thinking of the two earlier incidents, I said to Him one day, "Tell me about *Your* eyes." The immediate answer: "His eye is on the sparrow." I realized then that He kept telling me the same thing because He wanted me to know that His eye is on the sparrow and I can know He watches me.

Before our lives were interrupted by a threat to my vision, my and my husband Rick's desire had been for me to be known as a Christian artist—not just a nostalgic or realistic or Victorian artist, but a *Christian*

artist. We never would have imagined that an *affliction* would put a spotlight on my art and so clearly identify me as a Christian to those who know my work. But the Lord has used that affliction. And in this book He's used me to paint a picture. It is not a picture of a Christian whose maturity or knowledge was able to carry her through difficult days and months. It is a portrait of a plain, brown little sparrow who would have fallen to the ground without His care.

I haven't told you my story so that you could see me. I am only the sparrow. I share my story to help you see our heavenly Father, the One who is watching me—and you.

No matter what you're going through, if you really look for who He is, you will find Him watching you and caring for you.

Contents

Through Deep Waters

*I*am not surprised that I wrote a book. At least three people said to me that my experience would be a book. I am surprised, however, that I wrote *this* book! The book I wanted to write was about my healing. I do not say that lightly. I believe that God heals supernaturally today. From the very beginning, my personal preference was to experience instantaneous healing, as soon as possible. I never wanted to be the poster child for any kind of suffering!

Even as I encountered a threat to my vision, I sensed that God had allowed this crisis in order to give me a testimony to share. I expected that testimony to be healing, but healing did not and has not yet come. I was walking in "deep water," both physically and emotionally. My family kept hoping that we would "bottom out" in my situation. We were hoping that we had experienced the worst and that we would soon be on higher ground, on the other side of this serious crisis. As time went on and things got worse, not better, we found ourselves in still "deeper water." I found myself asking all the questions I thought I knew the answer to, and I wondered if I would ever be out of "deep water."

When two ladies from two different churches expressed an interest in my coming to their churches to give my testimony, I said to my husband, Rick, "I would love to go and give my testimony—as soon as I know what it's going to be!"

Do not fear, for I have redeemed you;
I have called you by name; you are Mine!
When you pass through the waters,
I will be with you; and through the rivers,
they will not overflow you.

ISAIAH 43:1,2

After walking in this "deep water" almost a year, though, it became apparent that God had, indeed, done a miracle in my life through His Word and that I do have a testimony. It is my testimony that He can replace fears, nightmares, and tears with rest and peace, although my problem still has no solution. And though my circumstances can still be described as "deep water," I am not drowning. I am walking on peace, joy, and confidence in the Lord.

There is a page in my Bible that has a note stuck to it. As our family was going through the early weeks of this trauma, my younger son, Jeremy, had come to me with a Scripture. That page in Isaiah is still marked with the note he wrote, "God did a lot for me with verses 1 and 2."

> *Do not fear, for I have redeemed you; I have called you*
> *by name; you are Mine! When you pass through the*
> *waters, I will be with you; and through the rivers, they*
> *will not over flow you (Isaiah 43:1,2).*

My friend Carolyn and I were driving through the scenic mountains of North Georgia one morning several years ago, and I tried to explain to her the new hunger for the Lord our family was experiencing. A new awareness of the Lord had been blowing through our house like a fresh breeze. We wanted more! "I would rather," I said (quoting someone else), "sink in the water headed to Jesus than spend the rest of my life in the stinking boat!"

And Carolyn said, "But I'm comfortable in the boat!"

More recently, Carolyn and I were discussing how much the Lord teaches us in hard times, and she reminded me of that earlier conversation. "Remember," she said, "you were the one who wanted to get out of the boat!"

She was right. But even though I had wanted to get out of the boat, I would have never volunteered to navigate this "deep water." At times I feared it would destroy me.

Now I can tell you that "deep water" is not to be feared. "Deep water" circumstances can be heart-rending and tempt you to despair, but it is in that same "deep water" that you can find the One who even the seas obey, if you look for Him. He can give you peace in the midst of the storm.

They say we can't leave footprints in water. But if you are hurting so badly that you feel you have lost your way, or even worse, that God has lost you, maybe my footprints through deep water can leave a path of hope and encouragement for you to follow.

Deep Water
BY KEVIN HARRIS

Take my life into deep water,
Where Your Spirit will rescue me.
Let me leave my shallow life behind.
Lord, I've searched so long and tried to find Your will for my life.
I'm casting out my nets on the other side.
Deeper is where my blessing lies.

Losing Control

The examination room was dark as the doctor examined my eye with a light so bright it temporarily blinded me. He said nothing as he pushed a probe against my eyeball and looked right and left and up and down. Finally, I broke the silence and asked, "What do you see?" His answer was, "Hemorrhaging." I knew that was never a good answer. And with his next words, "I need to call your husband in here. This is more serious than I was told," I walked into a nightmare.

I had gone to the doctor's office that after-noon expecting a simple office procedure. When I walked out, I had lost control of my life. I was scheduled for a surgery I didn't understand with a doctor I didn't know in a hospital I wasn't sure I liked. My schedule for the fall that I thought the Lord had planned so well was on hold. The doctor's diagnosis was a retinal tear and a retinal detachment in my right eye. Without surgery, that eye would be blind within two weeks.

> *Trust in the Lord with all your heart.*
> PROVERBS 3:5

This threat to my vision, even in just one eye, threatened so much of my life. I thought the Lord had called me to be a Christian artist. Would that come to an end? Would we lose our family business that is built around my art? It was hard for me to think of myself in any terms other than an artist.

The doctor had instructed me to go home and lie flat in bed until I returned for surgery thirty-six hours later. I couldn't even go upstairs. As I lay there in our guest bed-room, I noticed a flower arrangement I had ordered at the Christian Booksellers Convention a few weeks before. It had arrived in recent days and had not yet been hung in its place. I looked at that cluster of burgundy and yellow roses with a little ribbon that said, "Trust in the Lord with all your heart," and I thought to myself, "I don't know how to do that right now."

I was walking in a nightmare I could not find my way out of and encountering the first real suffering I had ever known. Though there was no real physical pain, the suffering was both psychological and emotional. As I tried to cope with what was happening to me, I was stalked by a spirit of fear, the fear of blindness. There were few days without tears and far too many nights with nightmares of going blind.

I wanted the Lord to do in me what He wanted to do in me, and I wanted Him to heal me. I tried my best to cooperate with both.

What about my call to be a Christian artist? The Lord obviously didn't need me to be an artist for Him. He could make an artist out of a stick! But I needed to paint. The gift He has given me can be used to bless others and honor Him. But it is also a precious gift to me.

For that period of time after the first surgery, though, there could be no painting, reading, or writing. I could only use my eyes to watch television at a distance. So I sat for six weeks being quiet and still and frequently checking for any sudden loss of vision. I wondered why courage was not one of the fruit of the Spirit! How did the Lord want to use this time? What did He want to say?

Seeing God

*E*arlier in the spring I had found a beautiful porcelain urn in an antique store in Texas. Immediately I knew I wanted to paint it full of magnolias. I hadn't planned any spiritual content for this painting. Without much thought or prayer I selected a Scripture to go with it. I was determined to finish this painting in record time, and I worked long hours. It was almost finished when my work was interrupted by surgery.

As I tried to recover, I sat in my studio day after day with this painting, not quite finished, in my view. It rebuked me—I wondered why I had worked like a driven woman on something that might never be finished. It made me sad—I wondered if I would ever be able to paint again. I even began using it daily as an "eye chart," checking my vision by trying to focus on the magnolias.

> *Blessed are the pure in heart, for they shall see God.*
> MATTHEW 5:8

In the sixth week, I was watching a video of an evangelist who mentioned the heart of the Son of God. I didn't really hear what he said next because, at that moment, an understanding of the purity of Jesus' heart was revealed to me. While I knew Jesus was too holy to overlook my sin, I understood for the first time that His heart was so pure that He was incapable of being offended at me and could not respond to me in a wrong way. I sat there in awe as I considered that kind of purity.

Two days later, I sat again in my chair with this painting in view and pondered what had been revealed to me about the Lord's pure heart. Suddenly, I knew my own need and my own desire. I needed a

pure heart—*His* pure heart. I immediately looked over at my painting and then remembered the Scripture I had chosen for it before my ordeal began: "Blessed are the pure in heart." I had been looking at the truth He wanted to show me for weeks, but I couldn't see it until He revealed it to me.

I was so excited that I told my husband, "I know what all this is for. Now I will get well."

In a week I learned I was worse, and in two weeks I learned I would need a more serious and delicate surgery to, once again, save my vision. Up to this point, I felt I had finally seen the Lord's hand in all of this. He had gotten my attention for some dusting and cleaning in my life, reminded me how I needed relationships with people, and revealed His pure heart to me. I could thank Him for my ordeal and count it worth it all. But not this. This is where I drew the line. I could not thank Him for getting worse.

As discouragement and frustration set in, my precious friend Gerrie, who has prayed through it all, suggested that maybe we would now see the rest of the verse: "For they shall see God." I knew how *I* wanted to see Him. I wanted the surgery to work, and I wanted to be healed!

But how did God want me to see Him? How does God want *you* to see Him? In your darkest moments, seek Him with a diligent heart. You will see God.

His Amazing Ways

Through all this I've found that God uses amazing ways to touch our hurting hearts. One of the special things that helped me was the way the Lord would bring old hymns to my mind that I had learned as a child.

Within a week of my first eye surgery, I had turned off the light and crawled into my bed one night only to discover that the light was still on—in my head. There was a bright green light glowing in the side of my vision with my eyes closed! Although the doctor's office later called this phenomena "normal," my brain told me it wasn't. As I waited for the mercy of sleep, the only escape I had from visual problems, more than one night I sang to myself, "The Light of the World Is Jesus."

When the doctors told me I would need a second surgery to save my vision, I made the mistake of asking exactly what they would do. In the weeks that I waited for surgery, the knowledge that they would enter my eye with sharp little blades called "daggers" tormented me with anxiety. I didn't have to be a rocket scientist to know what a little mistake would mean! As special friends and family covered me with prayer and fasting, I found the Lord was comforting me with the old hymns I knew. The day before the surgery, I awoke with, "Be not dismayed what e'er betide, God will take care of you," already in my mind. The morning I left for surgery, I awoke with "I need Thee every hour."

The Lord protected me through that surgery and the procedure was one of the most successful the doctor had ever performed. But as the weeks passed, it was apparent there were new problems. It is hard to find the words for the discouragement I felt. Not only had I not been healed, but I did not have the best results from modern medicine either.

I was so deeply distressed that I began to pray one morning and found I couldn't even pray. "Lord," was all I could say. There were not any other words there. I had prayed for so long—what else was there to say? And then, in the midst of my pain, there came to me fragments of an old hymn, "While life's dark maze I tread, and griefs around me spread, Be thou my guide, Bid darkness turn to day, Wipe sorrow's tears away…" I realized that this hymn was my prayer, and that when I couldn't even pray, the Lord had given it to me.

As the Lord used these hymns to comfort and encourage, I knew yet again that He was watching over me.

17

Sandy Plough

When God Is Silent

*T*here came a time when the encouraging verses and songs became very quiet. I was getting worse, and I wasn't hearing the Lord say anything.

I remember reading in Madame Jean Marie Guyon's book how she did not hear from God for several years. Her attitude was that she wasn't responsible for how God responded to her—only how she responded to Him. Before my trauma, it had felt so spiritual to share her story with others. But, it didn't feel very spiritual now. It was happening to *me*. And in spite of the ways the Lord had spoken to me, up until now I felt the only way I knew He loved me was that there were some people who were still praying for me.

> *My soul is in anguish. How long, O LORD, how long? Turn, O LORD, deliver me; save me because of your unfailing love.*
>
> PSALM 6:3,4 NIV

One thing I could not figure out was the source of my problems. Had Satan attacked my vision because I was a Christian artist?

Or, did it just happen to me because our flesh is weak and we live in a fallen world?

If this was a spiritual attack, we could stand in spiritual warfare against Satan and God could heal me. And if it had just happened to me, God could heal me.

A third possibility, suggested by some people close to me, was the one that almost devastated me. It was implied that perhaps God had not just permitted this to happen to me, but He actually intended it. Nobody said it out loud, but they implied that perhaps it was His will for me to be blind.

When friends said, "If you go blind, God is good" (which is a true statement), it sounded to me like, "If God makes you blind, God is good." Blindness was what I was terrified of. If God was causing my problem, then who would help me? Who could? And if God was willing for me to lose my sight, would I trust Him with my eyes? I was afraid. I was afraid of what God would allow to happen to me. I found I could not fear Him in that way and trust Him at the same time.

I believe that the devil took advantage of my situation and began to question God's character to me. It reminded me of Job's wife telling him to curse God and die. One of my friends who prayed with me wondered if I had given Satan grounds to attack my eye by having sin in my life. The Lord had done a dusting and cleaning in my life in the beginning of this crisis, and I had really tried hard not to have any unconfessed sin. I wasn't too proud to do another "checkup," but it made me feel a little like Job in the children's book my boys had when they were little. Job's friends said to him, "Job, Job, what did you do to make the Lord so mad at you?"

I had heard testimonies of people who absolutely came to the end of the road in their lives and cried out to God and He answered immediately. They were saved, healed, restored. Many times their cry for help included, "Lord, if You're real or really there—" Somehow, I felt like no matter how loudly I cried out, even if I had screamed and screamed for help, nothing would be any different. One night I thought, "Lord, from my circumstances

right now I would think that You're not there and You don't hear me. But I know You're there because You're there for other people."

Knowing that my emotions and my mind were not in line, I tried to put my will in line with what God wanted. But whenever I tried to consider that God might want me to lose my sight, it broke my heart. I could not find any peace.

Never being passive about finding some answers, I borrowed a book from my neighbor to study the names of God and to try to know His character better. I didn't get very deeply into this book when I ran into this verse, "And the LORD said to him, 'Who has made man's mouth? Or who makes him dumb or deaf, or seeing or blind? Is it not I, the LORD?'" (Exodus 4:11). I didn't know how to handle that verse. All I could think of was, "Who makes him...blind?" I closed the book. That was the end of that study for me. I just couldn't go any further. I wasn't finding the help and encouragement I needed, even from Christian friends and Christian books.

But I let what seemed to be God's silence draw me. I still searched for Him in my situation. He had not forgotten me, and He has not forgotten you. Search for Him with all your heart—He wants you to find Him.

God's Thoughts

Τ here is probably something each of us feels we could not survive losing: a mate, a child or parent, good health, a great job, a safe home. Such a loss might be too terrible for you to contemplate. As my younger son might say, you simply could not "go there." For me, it was blindness. I could not imagine surviving without my sight. I certainly did not want to end my life, but sometimes I was terrified of what living might mean.

> "For I know the plans I have for you," declares the LORD. "Plans for welfare and not for calamity to give you a future and a hope."
> JEREMIAH 29:11

On one of my darkest days, I had written in my journal, "On Sunday, I was so depressed the thought of hanging myself came to mind. This thought had never occured to me before. I knew this was a thought I could not afford to entertain. I knew that Satan wanted to destroy me." I'm so thankful that I *knew* those thoughts were not mine.

God's Word tell us that His thoughts are not our thoughts. Well, sometimes even what we think are *our* thoughts are not our thoughts! Thoughts of suicide are suggestions from the one who seeks to destroy us, when we are most vulnerable. These temptations are, as someone else has said, like birds—you can't keep them from flying over your head, but you can keep them from nesting in your hair.

You can do that by knowing that they are *not* your thoughts and certainly *not* God's, and they should be refused. God has revealed His thoughts toward me—and you—in His Word. Go there when those dark thoughts enter your mind.

When There Isn't an Answer

I was in the office of one of my doctors one afternoon for a test. I was optimistic that this test might provide a clue to solving one of my mysterious eye problems. As the doctor's assistant helped me, I told her about the terrible stress I had experienced during the last few months. Before I left, she came up to me and said, "You're a Christian woman. Just give it to God. All those weeks you were sitting and watching television you could have been praying for people."

I tried to explain that I was mostly watching Christian television and that I was asking God to do what He wanted to do in my life. She said again I needed to give it to God. I further explained that God had already protected me in two serious surgeries and that I believed He had an answer for me. Then she was in front of me asking, "What if there isn't an answer?" I didn't know what to say. "Well then," I finally responded, "I guess He will give me the grace for it." I left the office, all my optimism gone.

> *The counsel of the LORD stands forever, the plans of His heart from generation to generation.*
> **PSALM 33:11**

I made myself a mental note: *Never rebuke a hurting person.* As I thought about it later, I realized she had managed to accuse me and to accuse God by suggesting that I was a lousy Christian and God wasn't going to help me anyway! I knew I should disregard her behavior. But the question remained: "What if there isn't an answer?" I didn't want to consider that question. I had been waiting and hoping for a happy ending.

And I had other questions as well:

> Will God heal me?
> Why hasn't He answered my prayer?
> Is He even hearing my prayer?
> What would happen to me?

I had questions and no answers.

Her question hung in the air like a dark cloud over me: "What if there is not an answer?"

My friend Patti planned a dinner for Rick and me with her husband, Tom, and two other couples, Debra and Michael, our hosts, and Mark and Shelly. These wonderful new friends offered us fellowship and prayer. They had, as Shelly described it, "prepared a table in the wilderness" for us.

As we all sat around the table, Michael, in his kind way, shared some things he thought might be helpful to me. He had recently watched *The Hiding Place*, a movie about Corrie Ten Boom and her family, who were Christians during World War II. The Ten Booms hid Jews in their home in Holland. They were arrested by the Nazis and sent to a German prison camp. Corrie Ten Boom's father died shortly after arriving in prison. After much suffering and slave labor, her sister, Betsy, also died. Corrie Ten Boom's life was spared when she was released from prison due to a clerical error.

Michael reminded us that there was a change in Corrie Ten Boom while she was in prison. In the midst of her suffering and the loss of her beloved sister, she had changed from anger and bitterness to trusting God and ministering to others in peace and love.

Michael thought that perhaps whatever made the change in Corrie Ten Boom could help me find peace in the midst of my circumstances.

It had been years since I had seen the movie, so I took Michael's advice to heart and decided that I would watch it again. Four months passed before I actually did it. I think part of me hesitated to watch anybody suffering, as if it might be contagious.

I watched, rewound, and watched again the place where Corrie Ten Boom's heart was changed. I didn't want to miss a thing. She said, "Lord, put me in the center of Your will." I heard it, but nothing in my heart changed. So, a few days later, I watched the movie again. This time I saw a scene I had not remembered. As Corrie's sister, Betsy, in her weakened condition, sat on a lice-infested bed, she said to Corrie with a glow on her face, "Corrie, there must be a plan."

I knew the ending of their story. Corrie Ten Boom went all over the world, well into her eighties, telling how she had been to the pit and Jesus was deeper than the pit. There *had* been a plan.

From that time on, I knew in my heart there was a plan for me, although I didn't know what it was.

And even though I didn't know the answers, now I knew there was a plan.

Heal My Broken Heart

On my best days, I felt God was drawing me to a revelation of Himself. On my worst days, I wondered if I even knew Him. I had already made the agonizing choice to relinquish control of my eyes and give them to the Lord as my most precious possession. Although I had yielded my work, my life, my family, and my painting, this was the most difficult thing for me to surrender. But I realized that I had been holding onto something I did not have the ability or power to protect. Finally, one afternoon in my studio I told the Lord, "I don't just need my eye healed. I have a broken heart."

As for me, I said in my alarm, I am cut off from before Thine eyes; Nevertheless, Thou didst hear the voice of my supplications when I cried to Thee.

PSALM 31:22

I wanted to know for myself that God is good. I wanted to know what God says about Himself. I knew His Word was truth, so I decided to go to the book of Psalms. I got out a spiral notebook and at the top of the page I wrote, "The Goodness of God." Starting with the first chapter, I wrote down every verse that spoke to me about the goodness of God. If I didn't find what I was looking for in one chapter, I read until I found at least one verse about His goodness, even if I read four or five chapters. I still had those persistent questions: Why hadn't God answered my prayers? Did He hear me? What was going to happen to me? Would I ever be healed? But during the weeks I went through the book of Psalms, I began to be able to answer my questions with the Word. I realized that now I not only knew there was a plan—I had answers! I had answers from God's Word, and God cannot lie. These were not answers that told me what would happen next Wednesday or the next month, but they were truth. And that was wonderfully comforting.

Answers from God's Word

WHY HADN'T GOD ANSWERED MY PRAYERS? DID HE EVEN HEAR ME?

PSALM 4:3   *The Lord hears when I call to Him.*

PSALM 9:10   *For Thou, O LORD hast not forsaken those who seek Thee.*

PSALM 9:12   *He does not forget the cry of the afflicted.*

PSALM 66:20   *Blessed be God, who has not turned away my prayer, nor His lovingkindness from me.*

PSALM 116:12   *I love the LORD because He hears my voice and my supplications. Because He has inclined His ear to me, therefore I shall call upon Him as long as I live.*

PSALM 34:15-18 *The eyes of the LORD are toward the righteous, and His ears are open to their cry....The righteous cry and the LORD hears, and delivers them out of their troubles. The LORD is near to the brokenhearted and saves those who are crushed in spirit.*

IS GOD GOOD?

PSALM 25:6   *Remember, O LORD, Thy compassion and Thy lovingkindnesses, for they have been from of old.*

PSALM 26:3   *Thy lovingkindness is before my eyes.*

PSALM 25:8   *Good and upright is the LORD.*

PSALM 33:5   *The earth is full of the lovingkindness of the LORD.*

PSALM 34:8   *Taste and see that the LORD is good.*

PSALM 36:5   *Thy lovingkindness, O LORD, extends to the heavens, Thy faithfulness reaches to the skies.*

PSALM 86:5   *For Thou, LORD, art good, and ready to forgive, and abundant in lovingkindness to all who call upon Thee.*

PSALM 106:1   *Oh give thanks to the LORD, for He is good.*

PSALM 117:1,2 *Praise the LORD, all nations; laud Him, all peoples! For His lovingkindness is great toward us and the truth of the LORD is everlasting.*

PSALM 119:68   *Thou art good and doest good.*

WHAT IS GOING TO HAPPEN TO ME?
DO I HAVE A FUTURE?

PSALM 33:11   *The counsel of the Lord stands forever, the plans of His heart from generation to generation.*

PSALM 119:89   *Forever, O LORD, Thy word is settled in heaven.*

PSALM 138:8   *The LORD will accomplish what concerns me.*

PSALM 139:16   *Thine eyes have seen my unformed substance; and in Thy book they were all written. The days that were ordained for me, when as yet there was not one of them.*

PSALM 103:2   *Bless the LORD, O my soul, and forget none of His benefits; who pardons all your iniquities; who heals all your diseases; who redeems your life from the pit; who crowns you with lovingkindness and compassion.*

VERSES THAT EXPRESSED
MY OWN PAIN AND WERE LIKE PRAYERS

PSALM 69:16   *Answer me, O LORD, for Thy lovingkindness is good, accord-*
               ing to the greatness of Thy compassion, turn to me.

PSALM 119:49,50 *Remember the word to Thy servant, in which Thou hast made*
               me hope. This is my comfort in my affliction.

PSALM 119:82   *My eyes fail with longing for Thy word, while I say "When*
               wilt Thou comfort me?"

PSALM 119:107 *I am exceedingly afflicted; revive me, O LORD, according to*
               Thy word.

PSALM 119:124 *Deal with Thy servant according to Thy lovingkindness.*

PSALM 119:28   *My soul weeps because of grief; strengthen me according to*
               Thy word.

PSALM 119:74   *May those who fear Thee see me and be glad, because I wait*
               [hope] for Thy word.

PSALM 119:133 *Establish my footsteps in Thy word, and do not let any iniquity*
               have dominion over me.

PSALM 119:153 *Look upon my affliction and rescue me.*

Verses that promise rest

PSALM 29:11   *The LORD will bless His people with peace.*
PSALM 46:10   *Cease striving and know that I am God.*
PSALM 119:76   *O may Thy lovingkindness comfort me.*
PSALM 46:1   *God is our refuge and strength, a very present help in trouble.*

It didn't happen the first day or the first week, and it wasn't because of just one special verse. But as I went through these Scriptures, a peace began to settle in my heart.

Read them, meditate on them, hide them in your heart. Look to God's Word on your own. I encourage you to ask your questions and look to the only source of truth for the answers.

Why?

There are some questions we have trouble answering, even with Scripture. Every one of them begins with the word "Why?" Why do children die? Why do Christians lose their jobs? Why do their houses burn down? Why do people have cancer?

I sat at church one night watching an anniversary celebration honoring our pastor and his wife. Their older son, an outstanding Christian young man, had been killed by a drunk driver many years before. I saw their tears when this tender memory was mentioned, and I realized that even as they walk with a wonderful faith in the Lord, they must have questions. Even Corrie Ten Boom, at the end of her story of the Nazi prison camp, said that, still, there were questions.

> *Behold, the LORD's eye is upon those who fear Him, who wait for Him and hope in His mercy and lovingkindness.*
>
> PSALM 33:18
> AMP

I don't know why so many things went wrong in my eye. But more than knowing "why," I've needed to know that the God of the Universe is watching me.

We don't have to know "why" to find peace in the midst of our heartaches, and we don't have to know "why" to move beyond our trials. The truth is nobody really knows why.

The sparrow is a common, not very colorful, little bird. But this little bird is perhaps the most famous of all birds! Why? Because God wrote in His Word for all mankind to read: "Are not five sparrows sold for two cents? And yet not one of them is forgotten before God. Indeed the very hairs of your head are all numbered. Do not fear; you are of more value than many sparrows " (Luke 12:6,7).

He wanted us to know that He watches the plain little sparrows; He sees them—every one.

He also wanted me to know that He watches me, and He wanted you to know that He watches you.

Draw Me

BY RANDY NEWTON

How lovely is Your dwelling place,
My soul longs to see You face to face.
Even the sparrow has found a nest,
Lord, take my life to Your place of rest.
Draw me, draw me into Your courts,
For it's there I find my strength.
Draw me, draw me, into Your courts, into Your courts, into Your courts.
For there I will find my strength in You.

Enter Into Rest

After waiting four months for an appointment, we traveled to Johns Hopkins Hospital in Baltimore for a consultation with one of the very best neuro-ophthalmologists in America. We were very early for our appointment, and as we looked around, we wandered into the original part of the hospital, a wonderful, old, red-brick Victorian building. We entered a four-story rotunda, and in the center of it was a ten-and-a-half foot tall marble statue of Jesus with the Scripture carved into the base, "Come to Me, all who are weary and heavy-laden, and I will give you rest."

> *Come to Me, all who are weary and heavy-laden, and I will give you rest.*
> MATTHEW 11:28

I was amazed to find a representation of the Lord Jesus in the midst of all this science and research. I knew that many people, like myself, were desperate for help by the time they got to Johns Hopkins. I also knew that all of us would not find healing here but that we all needed rest. I was very touched to see that people had left flowers and notes and prayers addressed to Jesus on the base of the statue. Though as a statue it had no power or life, it was a powerful representation of the presence of the Lord.

After my appointment with the doctor, we went back to see the statue again. As I looked down to read one of the notes that had been left, my son Jeremy cautioned me that it might be too personal to read. I then noticed a note that had not been there before. It was in his handwriting. I asked him if he had left a note. He said "yes." Later he told me what it said. He had written, "Lord, we waited for four months and drove fourteen hours here to see the best doctor in the best clinic, and he can't tell us everything that's wrong. And he can't fix it. Father, You are our only hope. You are the Great Physician, and we're putting all of our faith in You."

I remembered the Scripture that says some trust in chariots and some in horses, but we will trust in the Lord our God. We left sobered but settled, knowing that Jesus is our hope.

Two weeks later, Rick and I returned to the retinal specialist I regularly see in Atlanta to discuss the findings of the doctor at Johns Hopkins. On this day we were put in a different examination room down a different hall from the area where we usually saw the doctor. Rick asked me if I knew where we were. I didn't. Then he pointed out that we were in the same room where this nightmare had begun. Although I made many trips to this office, I had not been in this room since the first day when another doctor had discovered how serious my problem was.

Then Rick asked me if I saw what was on the wall. I couldn't see it, so I got up and walked over to it. There was a photograph of the statue of Jesus at Johns Hopkins

Hospital with the Scripture, "Come to Me, all you who are weary and heavy-laden and I will give you rest." This photo had probably been here the first time I was in the room, but I had not noticed it.

Later I was talking to Jeremy about it. I told him that I knew it had a special meaning, but I wasn't sure what that meaning was. If *I* had been writing my story, this is where I would have been healed! I had come full circle, from the first day back to the same place almost a year later, complete with a picture of the Lord Jesus. What a perfect place for a happy ending to my story!

But I hadn't been healed. I told Jeremy that I just didn't know what my story was and what this meant. Jeremy replied, "Mother, this *is* your story. He has been with you since the very first day—even when you couldn't see Him." I realized that, indeed, God had used a statue and a photo of a statue to make sure I knew He had been with me and is still with me in this ordeal.

After almost a year of living in this nightmare, I realized that I had entered into a "rest." I had expected that a rest would be a "zip-pity-do-dah" kind of experience where my problems didn't bother me at all. But this was a rest where all my difficulties were still very real, but the fear and the torment had faded, and there was an emerging confidence that God had a plan. I saw a framed verse that described it very well, "Peace is not the absence of suffering, it is the presence of God in your heart."

If you're heavy laden, His presence can bring the relief of rest to you.

Finding "Normal" Again

Sometimes we begin our plans with, "When things get back to normal..." *Normal*—what a lovely, comforting, word.

We always hope that the storms in our lives will be temporary. After the storm has raged and the crisis has ended, we expect life to return to normal. I certainly did!

I wholeheartedly cooperated with my doctor's orders, expecting to get back to normal. But when the allotted recovery time was up, I wasn't normal. After waiting six stressful months, I wrote in my journal in utter frustration, "We all agree that my life needs to get back to normal. The problem is *I'm* not normal yet. I want to be normal again. I want to drive a car, I want to exercise, I want to see normally. I just can't accept that the handicap I'm experiencing is normal."

> *Do not fear, for I am with you; do not anxiously look about you, for I am your God....I will help you. Surely I will uphold you with My righteous right hand.*
> ISAIAH 41:10

But as I had lunch with my friend Patti one day at our favorite little Italian restaurant, I admitted to her, "Normal vision has become a memory." That was, I think, the beginning of realizing that there was no way I could get back to what I had been forced to leave behind. I had arrived at a new "normal." My "normal" had changed. It would change again and maybe again. But "normal" now is the new situation I find myself in—circumstances I am powerless to change.

Sandy Lynam Clough ©1995

Sometimes changes in our lives are temporary; sometimes they are permanent. Perhaps a death, divorce, illness, a move, or a job loss has separated you from the "normal" you long for. There is Someone you can bring with you to this not-quite-comfortable, new "normal," Someone who never changes. You can say, "Thank You, Lord":

You remain the same, and your years will have no end (Psalm 102:27).

For You are my hope; O Lord God, You are my trust from my youth and the source of my confidence. Upon You have I leaned and relied from birth; You are He Who took me from my mother's womb and You have been my benefactor from that day (Psalm 71:5,6 AMP).

As we adjust to circumstances we didn't choose but really can't change, we don't have to fear them because His "normal" never changes.

Courage To Keep Going

*T*he Atlanta freeways were almost peaceful at 5 a.m. the morning after the presidential election. Had the doctors who were scheduled to do my surgery stayed up as late as I had? For the first time, I wondered if they were Democrats or Republicans and if they were happy with the returns!

When we arrived at the hospital, it was still dark, and I had to force my feet to carry me inside where I had to, but did not want to, go. Have you ever had to do that? Have you had to force yourself to walk into a hospital, a funeral home, a courtroom, or even your own home? I not only wondered why courage was not one of the fruit of the Spirit, but I had no idea where someone like me could find it either.

My friend Ann, who is also an artist, has faithfully prayed for my healing for months and months. She told me one day that she knew people who had been inspired by my courage. You can imagine my surprise! I quickly assured Ann that I did not deserve credit for having any courage, because I really hadn't had any. If I really had courage, I felt I would face my problems like a fearless soldier, heroically running to the battle with my sword drawn, ignoring my wounds, never looking back, and certainly not going back. But Ann's comment got me thinking about what courage really is.

In the battles most of us are facing, there are only two options where being courageous is concerned—and turning around and going back is not one of them. We can choose to live through the days before us, or we can choose not to live. Choosing not to live is cowardly.

I was curious about Webster's definition of courage, so I looked it up. The first meaning listed read, "the attitude of facing and dealing with anything recognized as dangerous, difficult, or painful, instead of withdrawing from it." That sounds a lot like enduring to me.

When I was expecting my second child, I decided to be a real sport and try natural childbirth. As the moment of birth drew near and grew more painful, the doctor began to philosophize about how wanting to escape was a natural response for a woman in childbirth. I don't know about you, but I've never really known a woman in that condition—and that ridiculous position—who wanted to get up and run. Strangling the doctor might come to mind, but not running! I had no intention of leaving that delivery room. I had come to that place to leave with a new life.

What the doctor didn't realize was that I had already had one baby without doing anything to help, except to be there. And I knew that if I endured this time, new life would come forth—even if I didn't have the strength to help.

No matter what it is that brings you to a difficult place—death, illness, divorce, or even betrayal—God intends for you to leave it with new life. And it is not your own strength that will bring it forth.

So many days, as the morning sun streamed through the bay windows in our bedroom, I could see the floaters and spots in my eyes before I even opened them. And sometimes it has taken all the courage I could muster to open my eyes and get up and face that day and my problems. But if I don't keep going and meet each day, I will never experience the unfolding of God's plan for me.

Maybe that's what courage really is—deciding that no matter what happens you will keep going and enduring.

Fruitful in the Land of Affliction

When I was allowed to begin painting again, I was so grateful, but yet it seemed different. I could still do it. It just wasn't fun anymore.

One day Rick and I were talking on the phone to my father-in-law, a retired pastor. He said, "I've got a verse for you." As he had been reading his Bible, not looking or thinking about a verse for me, he had found this verse that he felt the Lord had given him for me: "God has made me fruitful in the land of my affliction" (Genesis 41:52). It wasn't a verse that said my trial was going to be over soon, but what a wonderful promise it was!

> *This is my comfort and consolation in my affliction: that Your word has revived me and given me life.*
>
> PSALM 119:50
> AMP

I fervently hoped my sojourn in the "land of affliction" was a visit and not a permanent relocation, but I realized I could not waste my time waiting for an exit visa! I made up my mind to use the "good eye" I had and trust God to multiply it like loaves and fishes. With this new enthusiasm, my joy in working returned.

Whether we find ourselves in difficult circumstances for a time or a lifetime, it doesn't have to mean lost time or a lost life.

Mourning into Dancing

As much of a relief as walking into a rest was, I wanted more. I needed more. I wanted to know God—to seek His face and not just His hand. I needed to *really* know what He is like and not just what He can do for me. To be brutally honest, too much of my Christian life had involved trying to use God for my own benefit—blessings, safety, healing, forgiveness.

> *My inner self thirsts for God, for the living God. When shall I come and behold the face of God?*
>
> PSALM 42:2
> AMP

I had finished the book of Psalms and writing about His goodness. I got my notebook and started again. This time I wrote at the top of the page, "You are wonderful because…" And what a wonderful Lord the Psalms described. What a picture!

PSALM 3:3,8	You are a shield for me, my glory and the lifter of my head…salvation belongs to you.
PSALM 25:6	You have steadfast love and mercy.
PSALM 89:14	You are due thanks for righteousness and justice.
PSALM 8:1	Your name is majestic and glorious.
PSALM 107:24	Your works are marvelous and your deeds are wonderful.
PSALM 135:13	You shall remain and continue forever.
PSALM 31:5	You are the God of truth and faithfulness.

PSALM 3:61	You are a refuge and a high tower for the oppressed.
PSALM 59:16	You are a refuge and stronghold in time of trouble.
PSALM 9:10	I can lean on you and confidently put my trust in you.
PSALM 11:7	You are righteous and you love righteous deeds.
PSALM 12:6,7	Your words and promises are pure words.
PSALM 16:2	There is no good beyond you.
PSALM 16:11	There is fullness of joy in your presence.
PSALM 31:21	Your lovingkindness is marvelous.
PSALM 18:2	You are my rock, my fortress and my deliverer, my God, my strength, my shield, the horn of my salvation, my high tower.
PSALM 18:30	Your way is perfect.

PSALM 19:7	Your law is perfect
PSALM 19:14	You are my redeemer.
PSALM 99:9	You are holy.
PSALM 29:1	You have glory and strength.
PSALM 29:4	Your voice is powerful and full of majesty.
PSALM 22:28	The kinship and the kingdoms are yours and you are the ruler over the nations.

Writing these praises were much more than saying, "I praise You, Lord." They were so wonderfully specific and descriptive.

My friends Patti and Florie came by one day to pick me up for lunch. When they came into the studio, I handed Patti my Bible and asked her to read this:

> *You have turned my mourning into dancing for me;*
> *You have put off my sackcloth and girded me with*
> *gladness to the end that my tongue and my heart and*
> *everything glorious within me may sing praise to you*
> *and not be silent. O Lord my God, I will give thanks to*
> *You forever* (PSALM 30:11,12 AMP).

The Lord had done that for me! When I had read that verse during my quiet time, I realized He had walked me from peace to rest and now into joy.

The God who tenderly watches over you can turn your mourning into dancing. He can walk you from peace to rest and to joy.

Dealing
with Setbacks

I went into my studio to begin my afternoon's work. Days earlier I had seen another Christian artist sharing his faith. It was a poignant reminder that I, too, had wanted to be and had chosen to be a Christian artist. But now it was no longer my choice. It was out of my hands. It was the Lord's choice. I can only paint as long as He gives me the vision to do it.

> I will praise the Lord no matter what happens. I will constantly speak of his glories and grace. I will boast of all his kindness to me. Let all who are discouraged take heart.
>
> PSALM 34:1,2

After I had painted a while, I noticed a strange spot in the center of my vision—not in my troubled eye but in the eye we affectionately call my "good" eye. "What is this?" I thought.

After walking in "rest," I had concluded that God would either heal my eye or so use my problem to His glory that I would be willing to live with it. If I had to, I could live and work with good vision in one eye and without useful vision in the other. We feared but did not anticipate problems in my good eye.

I reminded the Lord—I have no third eye! As I continued to work, this spot kept on losing focus. After I stopped painting, the spot disappeared in about two hours. Two specialists could find no physical cause for it. In tears of frustration, I said to the Lord, "Is it not enough that I have to work with distorted vision and double vision? Do I have to have this, too?"

As much as I didn't want to lose any more vision, I also didn't want to lose my peace. There were dark days of fear and torment behind me, and I didn't want to slip back into that. I continued to read my Bible looking for verses that said, "You are wonderful because," but one day I wrote in my notebook, "I have been dis-couraged. I wonder, what if I always get worse and my prayers are never answered? Am I foolishly optimistic for hoping in the Lord and believing He has a plan? When will a chapter in my journey begin without 'and then I got worse'?"

My verse for that day was waiting for me:

> *Why are you cast down, O my inner self? And why should*
> *you moan over me and be disquieted within me? Hope in*
> *God and wait expectantly for Him, for I shall yet praise Him,*
> *my Help and my God (Psalm 42:5 AMP).*

As if that wasn't plain enough, the same verse appeared again in the same chapter. And there it was again in the next chapter, this time adding: "For I shall yet praise Him, who is the help of my sad countenance and my God."

My hope restored, I offered a prayer of praise for what I was learning about my heavenly Father: "Lord, I praise You. I call You my help, I call You my stronghold, I call You my strong tower, I call You my mercy, I call You my righteousness, I call You my peace. You are the author of my life."

The next time discouragement reared its ugly head, I decided to go back to Psalm 42:5.

Thinking that reading it in another translation might make it fresh and more encouraging, I picked up my Living Bible. I had almost flipped to the right page when my eye fell on these verses:

> *I will praise the Lord no matter what*
> *happens. I will constantly speak of his*
> *glories and grace. I will boast of all his*
> *kindness to me. Let all who are discour-*
> *aged take heart (Psalm 34:1,2 TLB).*

I took heart. I wanted to be willing to trust the Lord—no matter what happened.

Sandy Clough

47

New Every Morning

The time came for the third surgery, and my family and I approached it with cautious optimism. The second surgery had caused a cataract that had damaged the lens in my eye. The lens would have to be replaced. It was intriguing to think that, just, maybe, underneath this cataract was good vision—and I had been healed after all.

> *O may Thy lovingkindness comfort me, according to Thy word to Thy servant.*
>
> PSALM 119:76

Before the bandages came off, though, I could tell that I had not been healed. The new plastic lens sharpened my vision, but my life just got harder, not better. The distortions and double vision became more distinct and dominant.

I was not a happy camper. Reading was almost impossible. I looked in the mirror and saw more clearly than ever one right eye and two left eyes. Would I ever know what I really looked like again? Putting on eye liner was certainly going to be a challenge! How could I work? I couldn't.

Though the deep despair was not there in this new round of difficulty, neither was my joy. I went back again and again to the verses that told me God is good. I did not want this trial to cause me to accuse God or to allow the enemy to misrepresent God's character to me. But still, sometimes I was afraid that no matter how hard I tried to keep painting and fulfilling my call, ultimately I might lose my sight, our business, and our living.

As I tried to find my bearings, I asked God to make me a blank canvas and to paint His image on me. However, I really did not want Him to use more suffering to do it. I felt like I had jumped off a cliff and landed in a new territory in the land of affliction. How could I learn to function here? The Scriptures that had helped me before seemed to belong to yesterday. This wasn't yesterday. This was today.

My friend Gerrie and I talked about how we need new "manna." Yesterday's spiritual food gives us testimonies and memories of God's special care, but today requires fresh food.

I realized then that I could not afford to miss my quiet time and reading my Bible. What if the Lord had a special verse He wanted to use to help me? If I didn't show up, I missed it. Some days were rich with verses that seemed to be written just for me. Other days, it felt like I was going through the motions. But staying in the Word had a cumulative effect of peace.

Fresh spiritual food might come from a friend, a song, or a sermon as well as God's Word, but we need it every day. Seek God's "manna" for you. Gather it. Be refreshed and nourished by it. My friend Florie quotes this verse so often: "His mercies are new every morning."

Who God Is

I vented my frustrations over this "improvement" in my vision to the doctor. His solution? He suggested I put cellophane tape over the lens of my reading glasses on that side. "Thirty thousand dollars in medical bills, and we're down to using cellophane tape," was my comment. But he was right. It worked, and I was back to work again. But I could not escape the reality of my situation. There was nothing else that medicine could do to help. The only healing possible for me now is supernatural.

> O Lord of hosts, blessed is the man who trusts in you.
>
> PSALM 84:12
> AMP

Gerrie's husband, Jerry, a pastor from Louisiana and our friend for over 20 years, called to suggest that Rick and I read two selections that he thought might encourage us from *My Utmost for His Highest* by Oswald Chambers. Rick got out our copy, and I located the two January selections. I quickly scanned them, and then I noticed another selection with several lines underlined. I was curious to see what I had underlined many years ago, and I was amazed. What I read was what I had been living: "Have you been asking God what He is going to do? He will never tell you. *God does not tell you what He is going to do: He reveals to you who He is.*"

As much as I have wanted one, there isn't a Scripture verse telling me what is going to happen to me. But the verses that have brought me peace, hope, and joy are the

ones that tell me about *Him*. Although He has not told me what He's going to do, He is showing me who He is.

With all my heart, I believe that my healing does not depend on me. It depends on who He is. What if I never get healed? The Lord is moving me away from speculation and trying to figure out what will happen to me and toward seeing Him. He is not calling me to live in "what if." He is calling me to live in "He is."

The Lord is calling you to see Him, too. Lay down the burden of speculation, the "what ifs" and "if onlys," and live in "He is."

When Others Fail You

There is probably nothing like a traumatic situation in our lives to keep us centered on ourselves. Sometimes my own need was so great, it almost seemed like I needed God to exist just for me. I know I felt so desperate that my attention rarely wandered far from what was happening to me and my eyes. My husband, Rick, patiently listened to my descriptions of the abnormalities in my vision for hours, days, and weeks. He gave hugs for tears and shared my frustration.

> *But the fruit of the Spirit is love, joy, peace, patience, kindness, goodness, faithfulness, gentleness, self-control.*
> GALATIANS 5:22,23

When we are hurting and fearful, the most wonderful people in the world are the ones who care about our problems through kind words, prayers, calls, notes, and hugs. When that precious attention is missing from a loved one, it's tempting to assume they simply don't care. I had seen other people almost abandoned by a family member when they needed them most. But I never thought it would happen to me. However, there was someone in my family who could not approach my pain or my suffering.

Rather than being with the family during my first surgery, he had gone to the mall shopping that day. As days passed into weeks, his visits became shorter. Some that could have been days were hours. He didn't

52

send cards, and he rarely even asked how I was when he called.

The absence of his expressions of concern and encouragement were painful to me. It felt like rejection. Sometimes I reacted to his outward behavior. Over time, though, the Lord showed me that if I wasn't careful, I could wound his heart deeply, because hurt people hurt people. The fruits of the Spirit—love, joy, peace, patience, kindness, goodness, faithfulness, gentleness, and self-control—are the only responses that wouldn't wound.

I also began to understand that this person I loved and needed could not approach my situation with outward compassion because he didn't know how. He simply didn't know what to say or what to do. He didn't understand that when we have no words, our very presence is still a ministry.

If you have experienced a death, divorce, or serious illness, you may be missing a dear friend or loved one who cannot come near to your pain. It may not be that they don't care, but that they don't know how to care for you. I encourage you to respond to their dilemma with love, joy, peace, patience, kindness, goodness, faithfulness, gentleness, and self-control. It will help you get through this time when you are loved, but from a little bit of a distance.

Working Together for "Good"

Most of us count on Romans 8:28, although we tend to overlook the second half of the verse that tells us *who* can count on all things working together for good. As Christians, we often seem to feel not just obligated but bound and determined to find the good in a bad situation, as if we needed to defend God.

I cringe inside when I imagine how many times women who have suffered miscarriages have had well-meaning people "encourage" them by suggesting that the "good" in the loss of a child was that there was probably something "wrong" with the baby anyway. One person looking for the "good" in my situation reminded me that Fanny Crosby was blind and wrote some wonderful hymns.

This kind of premature straining for good doesn't help hurting people; it only hurts them more. Romans 8:28 is true, but God has a timetable. It can take a long time before the good He has worked becomes obvious to us. It can be months, years, or even a generation before the good, like the last piece of a puzzle, helps things make sense. We simply cannot pull the "big picture" into focus by guessing how God will work.

> *And we know that God causes all things to work together for good to those who love God, to those who are called according to His purpose.*
> ROMANS 8:28

At one point, the doctors expected normalcy for me in two to three months. So as I prayed one day, I asked the Lord about shortening that time. I figured that since I should get better anyway, it wouldn't be a hard thing for Him to shorten the time and save me the stress.

He answered my prayer immediately with Hebrews 5:8, reminding me that His Son learned His obedience from the things that He suffered. I expected then to wait the full time. But when normalcy never came at all, I could see no purpose in what He was allowing to happen to me. I simply couldn't feel genuinely thankful for those dark days. How could He let me go through all that without intervening and rescuing me? Why would He allow difficulty to pile on difficulty?

It all seemed so frustrating and pointless—until many months later. My special friend Ruth suggested I write down how the Lord led me out of fear and frustration into confidence in Him in order to encourage others who were living without solutions to their problems. It was then that I saw a purpose in my struggles and could give thanks for that long nightmare. If you are going through a difficult time and you are encouraged, even a little, by how the Lord has helped me, you are holding in your hand my "good"—my evidence of Romans 8:28. God works the "good" in His time and in His way.

It is a waste of time for us to frantically look for good in a bad situation. What really helps is to look for God. Sometimes we can't see His hand working, nor can we force His hand. We need to be looking for His face, because it is His very character that will keep us in peace until the "good" is manifest.

A Personal God

From the very beginning, I wanted the Lord to give me or *somebody* a verse to hang onto. I wanted a verse that would give me hope and tell me what He was going to do. As I listened to a sermon tape one day, I heard a verse I didn't remember ever hearing before. It didn't tell me if I would be healed, but it expressed the desire of my heart, so I adopted it to be my special verse—what I hoped would be my outcome.

> *I had heard of You by the hearing of the ear*
> *but now my eye sees You.* (Job 42:5 AMP)

In the following weeks, that verse from Job became real to me. It did seem like I had only heard about God before, and now I was seeing Him with my spiritual eyes. A confidence in Him was emerging, but something was wrong.

There seemed to be a wall between the Lord and me. It was difficult for me to receive His love or express my love to Him. This barrier wasn't new. As I had struggled with it almost a year before, I had tried to put it into words in my journal: "There is something in my heart. I'm having trouble identifying it. Is it rejection? Is it unbelief? Whatever it is, it makes me feel removed from the goodness of God. That somehow the love and goodness of God doesn't connect to me."

I will not forget you. Behold, I have inscribed you on the palms of My hands.
ISAIAH 49:15,16

Almost thirty years ago I yielded my life to the Lord and began to walk with Him. I knew He had saved me, and I could tell you that if I had been the only person on earth, Jesus would have died for me. But I didn't feel that way.

Sandy Lynam Clough ©1995

Without meaning to sound irreverent, I felt like I was part of a "bulk purchase." John 3:16 says that God so loved the world that He gave His only begotten Son that whosoever believed on Him would have eternal life. That was me—"whosoever"—not "Sandy." The old hymn says, "Whosoever will may come." I was accepted because Jesus died for everyone. He died for "whosoever."

I knew Jesus loved me. He was so good to me. He had saved me and changed my life. He had blessed me and protected me, taught me and spoken to me. Yet, there was a hesitancy for me to boldly proclaim that Jesus loved Sandy and all of His promises were for her.

I have a good theological foundation. I understand "redemption" and "justification" and those other big words. I had all the facts. But when I considered the freedom and love other Christians enjoyed in the Lord, I felt like a second-class Christian who was missing out on something.

It was a sense of rejection that had resulted in unbelief. The Lord had not rejected me, and I certainly had not wanted to reject Him, but the feeling was there just the same. Rejection does not lead to faith; it leads to unbelief. It had also stunted my ability to worship and express love to the Lord. I had identified, finally, what the barrier was and wanted it out of my life.

I visited a Christian counselor, a longtime friend of our family, who has been blessed with discernment and wisdom. After sharing my concerns about rejection and unbelief, I shared my struggles in seeing the goodness of God and trying to understand suffering. "There are Christians who are almost crushed by their circumstances and God is glorified in it," I acknowledged. "But, in His Word, God is a refuge. He is loving and merciful. He doesn't call Himself a 'crusher.'"

"He crushed His Son for you," was the reply. He later said, "He was willing to be blind for you." After we prayed against rejection and unbelief, I was left alone. I thanked the Lord for His love, and I wondered if an awareness of His love would come to my heart like a flood. It didn't. It was quiet. And then Jesus spoke to me—not in a voice you could hear, but in my heart. I know it was His voice because the words were not mine: "I love you, Sandy." Jesus called me by my name. And then, "You're acceptable because I've made you acceptable."

One afternoon I said to the Lord, "How much do You love me?" I would not have been surprised if He had answered, "More than you know." I was surprised, however, at these words that He spoke to my heart, "More than you need." "More love than you need" for someone who had felt her own need was so great she almost needed the Lord to exist just for her! Just think—"more than I need"—and more than you need, too.

On Sad Days

I went to the mall one day to have some new glasses made. By this time, I was doing pretty well. I was resting in a confidence in the Lord and going on with my life full steam ahead. You could almost say I was "cruising." On the way home from the mall I was chatting with my friend, Patti, when I looked ahead and saw too clearly a normal truck with a truck shaped like a trapezoid on top of it. Although this visual distortion was certainly not new to me, I was seeing it so sharply that it might as well have been a billboard that said, "This is what happened to you."

> *Hope in God and wait expectantly for Him, for I shall yet praise Him, who is the help of my countenance and my God.*
>
> PSALM 43:5 AMP

By the time I got home, a heavy blanket of sadness had fallen over me. I wasn't depressed; I was sad. I wasn't even particularly discouraged. I still believed that God is good and He's working a plan for me. What I was experiencing was a fresh grief over what had happened to me. It wasn't self-pity. It was simply a sense of loss that was pointless to deny. It was a deep regret over the damage to my vision.

Whether we experience a death, a broken relationship, or some other personal loss, I think it is unrealistic to expect that we won't feel a sadness when something reminds us of that loss.

Even when we have confidence in the Lord's plans for the future, a loss of any kind is still a loss. Experiencing this sadness is not "backsliding."

I didn't know how to stop this feeling of sadness, so on the next day, I just followed my regular routine of reading God's Word. In a day or so my emotional equilibrium returned.

My Bible reading still included "You are wonderful because…" verses from the book of Psalms. It's important to me to keep going back to what God says about Himself. We hear a lot about what God will do for us and how He wants to prosper us. But the verses I'm finding confidence and comfort in are not so much about giving me "stuff" and prospering me as they are about God being what I need. For a while, I actually kept score to see which of the Lord's character qualities were mentioned most. The unofficial results? His mercy and then His lovingkindness were by far in the most verses, followed by His faithfulness, righteousness, strength, and truth. In many places I found He is my refuge, my rock, my salvation, my help, my shield, the one who hears me, and the one I can trust.

As I walk through my daily life there will probably be other situations and memories that will bring back a temporary sadness from time to time over my loss, but the Scriptures will still be there and they won't change. They will help me keep seeing the Lord as He is and not through eyes distorted by sadness.

It Is Enough

There seem to be two groups of people who believe that suffering can be a fertile garden of spiritual growth: those who have never experienced any suffering and those who have lived through suffering and survived. But for those of us in the middle of difficulties that seem to be without virtue or end, suffering is anything but a friend to be embraced. In fact, I experienced months where I felt like something was trying to destroy me physically and emotionally. The depth of the distress made the rest I found especially precious. It also made something else especially precious.

> For you have delivered my life from death, my eyes from tears, and my feet from stumbling and falling.
>
> PSALM 116:8
> AMP

What I had heard people call the "fellowship of His suffering" was a mystery to me. What was also a mystery to me was the concept that suffering could help me experience God's love. Frankly, walking through difficult days of distress did not make me feel like God loved me. I had trouble making the translation from suffering to love.

But it was those words, "He crushed His Son for you" and "He was willing to be blind for you," that opened a little window in my heart and helped me see.

I don't think God needs me to suffer for Him. I do think that the things I suffer help me see what He suffered for me. I have not experienced the sufferings of Christ—but I'm beginning

to understand that He has experienced mine and that He volunteered for it because He loves me. The depth of pain in my own meager suffering helps me see the depth of His love in His.

How many times have we heard ourselves saying to the Lord, "If You love me, why haven't You heard me and answered my prayers?" or "If You loved me, You would have protected me from what happened to me!" As if our Father could do anything more valuable for us to show His love than to give His precious Son. To ask for something else as proof of His love is to disregard His sacrifice.

My friend, Gerrie, lost a little grandson to cancer last year. When I asked her how she got through it, she said that she came to the point that Jesus had died for her and redeemed her and if He never did anything else for her—it was enough.

Do I still want the Lord to heal me? Oh, yes. But I cannot ask it as a proof of His love. Jesus did *everything* for me that I need on the cross. He knew when He suffered and died for me, that if He did that for me I would never need anything else. I do not pretend to understand everything He did when He shed His blood for me, but I know it was *enough*. I could have told you that before all this happened, but now I *know* it. And if you look for who He is, you will know it, too.

Although my path has been through "deep water" for more than two years now, the Lord has rescued me from the riptides of fear and distress and walked me into peace, joy, rest, and confidence in Him. The peace I found got my head above the water, and the rest He gave me helped me float on the deep water with splashes of joy. But what enabled me to walk forward with purpose and hope is a new confidence in who my Lord is and His absolute and personal love for me. I can't see the shore yet, but now, like Peter, I'm walking on my deep water. I'm not sinking in this deep water because my eyes are fixed on the Lord and not on the "what if's" of the waves.

Have you been introduced to a nightmare by a medical problem, an untimely death, or a divorce? Has your heart been broken by a betrayal, a move, or a wayward child? Just as seven skillful doctors could not end my nightmare, it may be that no human can change your circumstances and end yours either. Seeing my heavenly Father's heart ended my nightmare. He wants you to see His heart, too.

I no longer need to "camp" around my affliction and focus my life on it. In fact, I don't have time to camp there. I'm free and eager to get on to the hope and the future the Lord has for me. He has a hope and a future for you, too, you know.

If you are struggling with difficult circumstances that have no resolution, let the Lord tell you about Himself (even if you think you already know), and you will not drown in deep water. In fact, your footprints may leave a path for someone else who is crossing deep water behind you as you step into a new confidence in Him.

So do not throw away your confidence; it will be richly rewarded.

HEBREWS 10:35